THE POWER
OF LIVING FOR
GOD'S PLEASURE

THE POWER
OF LIVING FOR

GOD'S PLEASURE

CALVIN MILLER

TYNDALE HOUSE PUBLISHERS, INC.,
WHEATON, ILLINOIS

Visit Tyndale's exciting Web site at www.tyndale.com

Copyright © 2003 by Calvin Miller. All rights reserved.

Cover photograph copyright © 2003 by Michael Hudson. All rights reserved.

Designed by Jenny Swanson

Edited by Jeremy P. Taylor

Published in association with the literary agency of Alive Communications, Inc., 7680 Goddard Street, Suite 200, Colorado Springs, CO 80920.

Unless otherwise indicated, all Scripture quotations are taken from the *Holy Bible,* New Living Translation, copyright © 1996. Used by permission of Tyndale House Publishers, Inc., Wheaton, Illinois 60189. All rights reserved.

Scripture quotations marked NIV are taken from the *Holy Bible,* New International Version®. NIV®. Copyright © 1973, 1978, 1984 by International Bible Society. Used by permission of Zondervan Publishing House. All rights reserved.

Scripture quotations marked "NKJV" are taken from the New King James Version. Copyright © 1979, 1980, 1982 by Thomas Nelson, Inc. Used by permission. All rights reserved.

Scripture quotations marked KJV are taken from the *Holy Bible,* King James Version.

ISBN 0-8423-6173-1

Printed in the United States of America

07   06   05   04   03
5   4   3   2   1

Contents

PREFACE

The pursuit of happiness has become the great American obsession. But does any pleasure truly endure? There is nothing so inherently barren—nothing as cavernous and empty—as the pursuit of pleasure. At the end of every high school prom or wild spending spree comes the haunting question, "Is this all there is?" A great many heady romances end in the divorce court with the benumbed lovers shunning each other, made sick by the very sight of each other, and wailing in their lonely rooms, "I wanted more from life."

All of this shadowy disappointment is pushed forward on bright waves of secular promotion. "Try our cream, our crumpets, our credit cards, our confidence schemes, our infomercials. Then you will be truly happy!" We buy the delirium. We want to feel the pleasure. Surely someone must know what will make us happy. We ourselves have no idea. So we trust, mortgage, mail in, spend, and buy. We live in pessimism committed to optimism. The next big deal will be the one that will last.

Having given ourselves to the pursuit of pleasure, we watch our joys grow elusive and degenerate into the customary routines of dullsville. Then time and again we ask ourselves, "Where did my pleasure and happiness go?"

By midlife too often every dream of pleasure is finally dead. I'm convinced that many people go on measuring out their lives with broken hope.

This book sets out to answer one question: Is there a pleasure that endures?

If so, can that pleasure transform our lives? Yes! "The Lord takes pleasure in those who fear Him, in those who hope in His mercy" (Psalm 147:11, NKJV). God is incapable of being morose. The pleasure of God grows as his children delight in serving him. But there exists an even greater axiom of human happiness: only when God is pleased with us can we ever be pleased with ourselves.

The Hebrews used the word *shalom*, a word usually translated "peace," to signify their deep contentment with their God. His *shalom* never left them at the mercy of the world at hand. The Arabs have the same word, which they pronounce *salaam*. Menachem Begin said upon signing the Egyptian-Israeli Peace Accord, "No more wars, no more bloodshed. Peace unto you. Shalom, salaam, forever."[1] Faith in God's *shalom* puts him in charge of the tangled instances of our lives. We were made to love Christ, and our loving him pleases God. Then as his pleasure falls over us, we are given all the power we need to handle the strangling circumstances that choke the purpose from our dreams. This new sense that God is pleased with us dances his wonderful shalom into our souls. God smiles and we are set free from the shackles of believing that what anyone else thinks matters. We live for God's pleasure alone.

This wonderful feeling of rightness—this deep, abiding shalom—comes as a special prize of the pleasure of God. God has smiled! No matter then if all the world should frown at us. When God is pleased with us, who could ever keep us from finding self-worth? God wants us to live beneath his smile. He wants us to feel the pleasure he takes in our obedience. So shalom has two sides—a heavenly side and an earthly side. Pleasure is God's side of the great shalom. Joy is our side. When the pleasure of heaven lights our days, joy becomes our way of life. In God's wonderful shalom, we wake to wonder. The sky is bluer, the earth is greener. Symphonies become the soundtrack of our ordinary days. The dirge becomes a mad dance. All bread is cake. And our ritual sunrise worship is this: "Hallelujah thou great Shalom! Is all this for me, God?"

God's pleasure and our joy are the two great chords in the symphony of transformed living. Jesus himself is the Master of the Dance, and the joy we feel comes directly from the pleasure God takes in our obedience. Morning by morning there is manna on the ground. Evening by evening, we hear the king of heaven inviting us to a fling of joy. We have obeyed, God has smiled, the music flies!

"On with the dance! Let joy be
    unconfined;
No sleep till morn, when Youth and
    Pleasure meet
To chase the glowing hours with flying
    feet."

Lord Byron, Childe Harold's Pilgrimage, *Canto iii.,
Stanza 22.*

• • • •

ELIJAH
A STUDY
IN PLEASURE
AND POWER

Elijah was a person of power. His name is a gathering of Hebrew particles that, when assembled, mean, "God is the LORD." Elijah took a lonely stand for God in a most unpopular place. His foes were the four hundred and fifty prophets of Baal who lived at the queen's court. All of these worshiped the easy, accessible gods of money and sexual indulgence.

WHEN WE WIN GOD'S PLEASURE WE RELEASE WITHIN OURSELVES THE POWER TO ACHIEVE.

Baal was a calf of gold. He lured his adorers to seek wealth. But he was not so much a calf as he was a pagan bull conferring sexual indulgence on the lusty and self-willed souls who bowed at his altar.

Elijah preached the great God of requirement. Yahweh was his covenant name, and he demanded self-denial and the high adoration of surrender and confession. So when the confrontation came, Elijah stood on the mountain to cry to his idolatrous culture: "How long will you falter between two opinions? If the Lord is God, follow Him; but if Baal, follow him" (1 Kings 18:21, NKJV).

Elijah and God were a force of two. They were far outnumbered by the priests of public opinion. Elijah challenged the prophets of the false god to a duel. The prophets of Baal set their sacrifices before their golden bull. Elijah laid his sacrifice before Jehovah. The gauntlet of the gods was cast. The god who answered by fire would be God.

God smiled above his gallant and fearless, willing-to-stand-alone prophet. There were flames everywhere—flames that lapped up even the water in the trenches. And the pleasure of God awoke a storm of power within Elijah. The fire fell! God smiled on! Elijah ran ahead of Ahab's chariot all the way to Jezreel.

When we win God's pleasure, we release within ourselves the power to achieve. Elijah won God's pleasure, and it released in him the power to run. But how do we win God's pleasure? Exactly as Elijah did. We agree to obey even at those moments when obedience requires everything of us. For Elijah, to obey was to stand alone, to risk the forfeiture of his life.

Let us enter into the exciting world of godly obedience. Our obedience will win the smile of God, and the smile of God will give us the power to make our world an arena of self-confidence. Always? Yes—no matter what our obedience may cost us! For it is impossible to think ill of ourselves when God is smiling on our obedience. In fact the entire Bible is a collection of true tales of men and women possessed with the idea of pleasing God.

Noah built a boat in the midst of ridicule and won the pleasure of God.

Esther risked her life to know his pleasure.

Stephen cherished truth in the face of flying stones and won the pleasure of God.

There are many virtues that grow out of

4

our obedience. Joy, peace, and gratitude are three of the best. But perhaps the finest evidence of our obedience is self-confidence. When I am in business solely to serve and please God, his smile settles on me as power.

I am not talking here about the power of the Spirit. That is power indeed and always comes as a companion force to the power of his pleasure. The power of the Spirit falls upon us to enable us to widen his kingdom and serve the world Christ died to save. But the power of God's pleasure is the power of a vibrant attitude that gives us a radiant winsomeness while we serve the Spirit. So for now let us talk of obedience power. I have but to obey to win his pleasure—then hell sways weakly in my pathway. I, who am only me, am more than me.

I am on Mt. Carmel.
I take my stand.
God smiles.

I became the final extension of his smile.

I can do all things through Christ.

All things? How? What makes it happen?

God is smiling.

The world is wax before such a flame.

• • • •

INTRODUCTION

* * * *

When I feel the presence of God, it feels like drafting a big truck. It feels like my prayer goes from being pushed along by a little put-put engine to being pulled by a monster diesel. The reason prayer feels like drafting a truck rather than just getting a bigger engine is that when I feel the presence of God, it feels like I am being pulled by something that I'm close to but can't touch. My feet are still on the ground, but I feel like I am being lifted. My steps feel lighter. I walk faster but much less deliberately. My thinking focuses. Far from being an irrational, ecstatic phenomenon, in this state my rational process leaps forward from point to point, as if I am bounding through a field of high grass on the back of a lion, holding his mane and laughing with glee. No matter what I was praying about, whether I feel an answer or not, all I can do is praise and thank God. I always think best when I am worshiping God.

—DAVID HANSEN[2]

* * * *

THE PLEASURE OF SERVING GOD

To serve God is to serve others. There is nothing we can do for God directly. What could we possibly draw from our crude hovels to furnish his palace? This world's millionaires are heaven's lepers. If we would please him, we must serve not only those whose needs are convenient for us to address but also those whose needs are greater than ours—we must serve all who are within the reach of our supply. *Do* instead of talk, said James (James 1:22). Don't call me Lord without obeying me, said Jesus (Matthew 7:21). "Give generously, for your gifts will return to you later," says Ecclesiastes 11:1. God is so much in love with us that we have but to serve him in the most modest of ways to be sure that we have pleased him.

We win the pleasure of God through ministry. Teresa of Calcutta speaks for the Christ of Matthew 25. To do any needful thing in the name of love is to do it unto Jesus. Bandage a leper, and you swathe the Son of God. Feed the starving a bowl of steaming soup, and the meal is served piping hot to Jesus.

I have a missionary friend who serves in Calcutta. During Mother Teresa's final years, he actually had the opportunity to visit with her. He noticed after one of their talks that many of the homeless of Calcutta were insane. There were no hospitals for them. They lived pretty much as they had in medieval times. They wandered the streets at midnight in search of bread. So this missionary began buying loaves of day-old bread. When he saw homeless people approaching, he scattered the loaves in the streets where they would

> IF WE WOULD PLEASE HIM, WE MUST SERVE NOT ONLY THOSE WHOSE NEEDS ARE CONVENIENT FOR US TO ADDRESS BUT ALSO THOSE WHOSE NEEDS ARE GREATER THAN OURS.

shortly pass. His delight came in seeing them discover the food. When they did, they greedily ate. His unseen feeding of these mindless men and women filled him with the sensation of Matthew 25:40, "I assure you, when you did it to one of the least of these my brothers and sisters, you were doing it to me!" He learned Mother Teresa's lesson. It wasn't the demented guttersnipes he fed at midnight, it was the Son of God.

He discovered a liberating truth. This is heaven's blessed paradox: Christ can do anything, yet he waits on us to give him hands. He has forgone the use of his own hands to get things done. Jesus, the all-powerful, has willed himself to be the Almighty Amputee of Heaven, waiting for us to give him hands so he can serve his starving family. He graces us with his dependency. Yet how frequently we leave him handless. How rarely we reach out to others. When we do, our hands are often claws of greed. We use them to rake the good stuff of life into our own glutted accounts and bulging treasuries.

Materialism has become the obstruction in our pathway to God's pleasure. We are both our old, preconversion, selfish selves and God's new child living together in one conflicted soul. "I do not understand what I do," said the apostle Paul. "For what I want to do, I do not do, but what I hate I do. . . . Now if I do what I do not want to do, it is no longer I who do it, but it is sin living in me. . . . What a wretched man I am!" (Romans 7:15-24, NIV). Wretched are we all! James said we are double-minded. We want to serve God, but we also want to "do our thing" for our own achievement. James' word for double-minded really means two-souled (*dipsuchos*, James 1:8 NIV). Shakespeare's Gertrude saw that she was double-minded and freely admitted to Hamlet, "O, Hamlet, thou has cleft my heart in twain." Hamlet well advised her, "O, throw away the worser part

of it, and live the purer with the other half"
(III, iv, 163-165).

Hamlet has our number: we are ever two
people. The first and worst is committed to
our own pleasure. The second is committed to
God's pleasure. It is important to decide
which of these two selves we really are.

> Within my earthly temple, there's a crowd;
> There's one of us that's humble, one
>   that's proud;
> There's one that's broken-hearted for
>   his sins;
> There's one that unrepentant, sits
>   and grins;
> There's one that loves his neighbor
>   as himself
> And one that cares for not but
>   fame and self.
> From much corroding care I
>   should be free
> If I could once determine which is me."
>   —EDWARD SANFORD MARTIN[3]

FINDING THE LIFE OF JOY

The trick is to find and serve with a life that is in tune with Christ. Then we can find the life of joy. It will then be a life God fills with power. The power that fills us will come directly from God's pleasure. You may expect it, for true pleasure is always to be found in our nearness to him. The psalmist makes the point: "You will show me the way of life, granting me the joy of your presence and the pleasures of living with you forever." (Psalm 16:11). We cower before God in wholesome fear, and yet we hungrily seek him as we fear him.

PRAISE IS THE ONLY MUSIC EARTH CAN FURNISH HEAVEN.

F.B. Meyer, the great nineteenth and early twentieth century theologian, realized that Ecclesiastes 12:13 is right: we are to fear God and keep his commandments. This is the whole duty of man. Until we pass uncomfort-

CALVIN MILLER

ably close to God's power, we really do not
believe in it. Only as we fear him, do we
believe in him with understanding. Meyer
wrote these words:

> They love thee little if at all who do
>   not fear thee much,
> If love is thine attraction Lord,
>   fear is thy very touch.
> We love thee because thou art so
>   great and because we sin,
> And when we make most show of love,
>   we tremble most within.

How true! We cannot please God without
being filled with his awesome power! Until we
set his almighty strength alongside our
almighty need, we cannot take the first step
toward his almighty pleasure. How glorious
his nearness. Our wholesome fear of his presence will soon fade into an intoxication with
his nearness.

As King David of Israel lay dying, he craved more than ever a final nearness of God. He found this longing for nearness to be the gates of eternal pleasure, which he was soon to occupy. He prayed, "I know also, my God, that You test the heart and have pleasure in uprightness. As for me, in the uprightness of my heart I have willingly offered all these things; and now with joy I have seen Your people, who are present here to offer willingly to You" (1 Chronicles 29:17, NKJV).

> WHEN WE SEEK GOD'S PLEASURE, WE FIND A LIFE FILLED WITH THE JOY THAT CAN COME ONLY FROM PLEASING GOD.

David, through years of trial-and-error obedience, had discovered that God could actually take pleasure in human flesh. He knew that the way to win the smile of God was to please him with a clean mind and an upright heart. "Who may climb the mountain of the Lord? Who may stand in his holy place? Only those whose hands and hearts are pure . . ." (Psalm 24:3-4). In Psalm 51:10 he wrote, "Create in me a clean heart, O God." David also knew that out of a clean heart he could offer the purest praise, and win pleasure—the purest pleasure of God. So the poetry of the psalms became his path of pleasure and praise, and thus, his point of entry into God's abiding presence.

Why poetry? Because, the ordinary, poorer verbs and nouns of everyday language were too small an offering for the preeminence of God. So the psalms became David's way to express praise. Praise is the only music earth can furnish heaven. David understood. When we adore the Father, we become for him the child who is worth the cost of salvation. In praise, we are all prodigals come home. We are all rebels restored! We are the lost pearls of great price, stuffed once again in the treasure trove of God. Our obedience brings us to the table of his presence—to the gold damask of the banquet tables of God.

Nothing compares with this rich intimacy.

David had once pursued carnal pleasures with Bathsheba. He had learned the hard way that when he pursued pleasure for his own enjoyment, God was forgotten. His need taught him praise. He found that when he praised, God turned his face to him in pleasure. And when God looked upon him with pleasure, he looked upon his world with joy, and met his human involvements with moral and personal righteousness and power.

Praise him, please him.

Please him, and the power of his pleasure is yours.

Joy will come as a proof that he is pleased.

So joy is never something you achieve with practice. Drive too hard for it, and you will miss it altogether. Joy is the by-product of your desire to please God. Win his smile, and joy will be dumped on your obedience by the bucketful.

The writer of Proverbs said, "Those who love pleasure become poor (21:17)." Pursue pleasure and it will elude you. But seek God, and joy, the by-product of his pleasure, will be yours in abundance.

This book is based upon the certain knowledge that when God smiles down on us, that glorious approval carries with it a deluge of joy. When we seek God's pleasure, we find a life filled with the joy that can come only from pleasing God.

THREE STEPS TO THE POWER OF GOD'S PLEASURE

God's smile floods all reality with light. When God smiles, our world is lit beyond all imagining. In such light we see who we are (our identity) and where we are to walk (our calling) and how we are to treat those who have not yet seen the light. In such light we lose all selfish interest

in pursuing earthly pleasure, for a better pleasure will have already apprehended us.

But how does this happen?

There is only one path to the power of his
pleasure. It consists of three steps.

**First, we must see God as our Father,
a Father who is capable of pride or
disappointment in us.**

Until we see God as a real person who feels
pride in our obedience and experiences the
pain of our brokenness when we rebel, we will
live outside his plans. We cannot in such a
state bring God pleasure.

**Second, we must be honest enough to
admit that our own mood is determined
by how God feels about us.**

The way to truly care about how God feels
toward us is to realize that God's feelings
determine our own feelings. Once we realize
that God's pleasure or disappointment in us

creates in us feelings of exuberance or depression, we will begin to hunger to obey him.

The third step is realizing that power for living is the product of God's pleasure.
Our service and God's pleasure are closely related. But what can we do that might bring God pleasure? The overwhelming majority of Christians have never taken the time to discover what it is that God has for them to do in life. They plan careers, develop jobs, acquire employment, even start families, all without ever taking the time to ask God what his will for their life is. In fact, most Christians never believe they have a calling.

HEARING AND HEEDING GOD'S CALL

The call! Who can deny its glorious, life-long power over us? I came to know Christ in 1945, when I was nine years old. Our friendship was my treasure. I could scarcely pass an hour of time without exulting in his love.

But when I was fifteen, I realized that his love was not a bubbly spa of giddy infatuation. He had a world to run, a race to redeem, and continents to heal. Then I knew that love was not just the pastime of God, it was the business of God, and I must play my part in his business.

But what was I to do?

We find our call in the midst of a great deal of inner wrangling. And in the path of claiming our call, we argue a lot with our inner selves. My argument centered around how I was to find the most fulfillment from my life vocation. If I became an architect, whatever building I built would in time fall down. If I became a doctor and saved lives, I could not save them forever, they would soon die of some malady in spite of my effort to

> **THOSE WHOSE EVERY WORKING, WAKING MOMENT IS GOD'S HAVE FOUND THE SECRET OF INTEGRATED JOY.**

save them. There was only one pursuit my life could take where everything I did could be saved until eternity: a career given to Christ.

Thus my call was established, and as with any facet of the will of God, once I agreed to God's design, my life fell into peace—the peace that comes from the concord of our agreement with the Almighty. I also felt a great deal of inner power, for I had pleased God, and knew the power that comes from his pleasure.

Peter Marshall referred to his call as the tap on the shoulder, the tap that says, "I want you." When he agreed to the "tap," he too felt the power of God's pleasure.

Too many Christians believe that their faith is one thing and their employment is another. How sad! Those who believe these two items could never have the slightest relationship divide their souls and split their lifestyles. For all the rest of their lives they worship in one place and work in another, never seeing any connection between the two.

But there is a dimension of life in Christ where the worship place and the work place become one. Brother Lawrence, a seventeenth century monk, made the monastery kitchen his prayer closet. He married his prayer life to the scrubbing of pots and pans. He wrote, "There is not in the world a kind of life more sweet and delightful than that of a continual conversation with God."[4] What better way to carry on a continual conversation with God than to allow God into our workplace? God was available to Brother Lawrence anywhere, anytime, for he never allowed his workplace to be separate from his worship place. The dish tub may be an altar when the heart is centered on God.

For me, I had to learn to sanctify every moment. Jean Pierre de Cassaude taught me to look at the world in such a way that every object my eyes fell upon was an altar. There I met the Father; there we talked. Wherever I worked—and I worked for years in a factory—there was my altar. There I worshiped. All I had to do was sanctify my world, and the present moment was my time with him—whatever my hands were doing, wherever I happened to be working. Those whose every working, waking moment is God's have found the secret of integrated joy. They live beneath the pleasure of God. They derive the power to shape their lives directly from his pleasure.

Your joy and his pleasure come and go together in life. If you have either, you will have both.

So come let us reason together.

Let us advance through these pages.

Certify God's dimensions of glory.

Get ready for an adventure.

There is but one way to live:

The Savior must have pleasure in you.

You must know the power of his ongoing joy.

Please him, praise him, wake to wonder.

"While with an eye made quiet by the
   power
Of harmony, and the deep power of joy,
We see into the life of things."

WILLIAM WORDSWORTH,
Lines Composed a Few Miles Above Tintern
Abbey, *stanzas 46–48 (1798)*

• • • •

CHAPTER ONE

SEE GOD AS YOUR FATHER, CAPABLE OF PRIDE AND DISAPPOINTMENT

❋ ❋ ❋ ❋

*Once, as I rode out into the woods for my health,
in 1737, having alighted from my horse in a
retired place, as my manner commonly has been,
to walk for divine contemplation and prayer, I
had a view that for me was extraordinary, of
the glory of the Son of God, as Mediator between
God and man, and his wonderful, great, full,
pure and sweet grace and love, and meek
and gentle condescension.*

—JONATHAN EDWARDS[5]

❋ ❋ ❋ ❋

LIVING FOR GOD'S PLEASURE

Most Christians live in weakness, never knowing the power of God's pleasure. The reason for this unfortunate reality is obvious: they have never seen God as capable of heavy "human" emotions toward them. Is God human? Of course not. No more than a mere human could ever be divine. But God is a person. He knows all the emotions of being human. He created human emotion, and he enters into relationship with us humans.

How he feels about us, therefore, should be understood in the same way we feel about him. Do we feel pride and love? Of course! God has these same feelings toward us.

Scripture abounds with references to God's feelings. There are more than one hundred verses that speak of God's being pleased with us or taking pleasure in our obedience. But I would like to focus on just one: "Do not fear, little flock, for it is your Father's good pleasure to give you the kingdom" (Luke 12:32, NKJV).

Like any parent, God feels joy when he is able to give his children the gifts he longs to lavish upon them. Our obedience releases in us his most pleasing gift—the power of his pleasure.

> LIKE ANY PARENT, GOD FEELS JOY WHEN HE IS ABLE TO GIVE HIS CHILDREN THE GIFTS HE LONGS TO LAVISH UPON THEM.

How powerful is his pleasure? People who believe they are pleasing God accomplish two things. First, they feel good about themselves. Second, perhaps without even knowing it, they help change the world for the better. Every time a disease is eliminated, a war truced, a temple erected, a bridge built, or a child rescued, someone, somewhere is confident he has made God smile. God's smile sets ordinary mortals down at the banquet of the Father. "Let there be sung 'Non Nobis,' " said Henry V, referring to the Latin hymn *"Non nobis*

Domine, sed nomini, tuo da gloriam." Not to us
O Lord, but unto you be all the glory.

An old man who swept the flourmill floor
in my hometown paid for my second year of
college anonymously. I received it, but I did
not know for thirty years who gave me such
a gift. I met this silent benefactor at mother's
funeral. By this time he was a very old man.
My eyes filled with tears as he said to me (in
English of course), *Non nobis Domine, sed
nomini, tuo da gloriam.* "Look up to God, he
has furnished this feast, and you were worth
every mouthful of joy that God gave me to
devour." I have been warmed often by the
power of the old man's pleasure, for I knew it
was the power of God. He was convinced he
had done nothing admirable—he had but
obeyed God. It was the only course open to
him as an obedient child. His obedience had
brought him great pleasure because it had
brought God pleasure. The pleasure of the
Father is all that matters.

HURTING THE HEART OF GOD

Our obedience brings God pleasure, which brings us pleasure. Conversely, when we are disobedient, we hurt God. It took me a long time to realize that God didn't just get mad when I sinned; he was hurt. Perhaps we have to have children of our own to truly realize this. I'm not sure that our children ever see that their sin does not anger their parents so much as it hurts them. When we finally do understand this, often not until adulthood, we take a giant stride in our maturity.

The apostle Paul begs us not to hurt the heart of God. "Do not grieve the Holy Spirit of God," he says, "by whom you were sealed for the day of redemption" (Ephesians 4:30, NKJV). Grieve is a love word, not a term of judgment. That is to say, that our indifference to what God wants from us does not make him mad, it injures him. That is not to say he will not punish us; he will. But before we ever stir his indignation, we call forth his tender love. We break his heart in grief before we ever make him angry.

How foolish we are to fear his anger. We have far too much trembled before the "God's gonna get you" syndrome.

My mother, who raised me and my eight other siblings, mostly as a single parent, was a believer in chastening us children. Chastening in Oklahoma was called "gettin' a lickin'." We feared making her mad, for it always seemed to be hazardous to our health. It seemed that when she came through the door with a plaster lath or a peach switch in her hand, it was wise to pray fervently for the Second Coming. Better history should end than our frail lives.

As I grew older, I began to sense that following our tears, it was she who was really crying. The odd sensation of seeing my mother cry became the best incentive to my good behavior. I hated to see her cry. While her smile was the diamond at the center of all my self-esteem, her tears were terrible to me.

I needed her pleasure to live. I spent it like hard cash to purchase my joy. I eventually came to the place where I outgrew the "momma's gonna get you" fear. I replaced it with, "I will never again hurt this wonderful, self-giving person." I literally lived to bring her pleasure.

So it is with God.

In every moral choice, we have not merely our own disappointments to consider. In our every choice we either grieve or please God. God is our Father, and he is always grieved by our selfishness. While he is in this state of grief, we live powerless lives, marked by no effervescence of spirit.

But when we are broken, we elicit the pleasure of God. "The Lord is close to the brokenhearted," says the psalmist (Psalm 34:18). Indeed he caresses their pain until it is transformed to joy: "He heals the brokenhearted, binding up their wounds" (Psalm 147:3). Our own contrition always precedes our joy. Why?

Because "The sacrifice you want is a broken spirit. A broken and repentant heart, O God, you will not despise" (Psalm 51:17).

GOD'S GREATEST GIFT

It is our Father's good pleasure to give us the kingdom. What exactly elicits God's greatest pleasure toward us? Our receiving his gifts! Consider Christmas. When my children were small, they thought they were excited about Christmas, but their excitement could in no way match my own. As a father, I lived for those first early moments around the Christmas tree. Their excitement at receiving could never match the sheer ecstasy I felt in watching them receive my gifts.

God's greatest gift to us is his kingdom. The word *kingdom* itself is one of those "grace" words. Who can inherit a kingdom? Only the son or daughter of the king, of course. But God is giving you his kingdom! So to say the word *kingdom* is to realize that God's gift to you is to see yourself as a brother or sister of Jesus, the crown prince of the kingdom. Contemporary Christians seem to have lost the idea that Jesus is the King and they are brothers and sisters, princes and princesses of this kingdom. I particularly remember the evangelist who first led me to Christ. He preached the King and his kingdom. So I entered instantly believing in my King, my Sovereign and brother. I received this kingdom first as a child and have been living in it ever since. I was a child when I became a subject in his realm—in this never ending glory we call the kingdom of God. Was God present? Yes. Did he feel joy? He was ecstatic with the pleasure he felt as I unwrapped this greatest of all

> PEOPLE WHO BELIEVE THEY ARE PLEASING GOD FEEL GOOD ABOUT THEMSELVES AND, PERHAPS WITHOUT EVEN KNOWING IT, HELP CHANGE THE WORLD FOR THE BETTER.

presents, the kingdom of God. It was his good pleasure to make of that ordinary day a grand Christmas, whose delight continues to thrill both me and him.

It thrills me just because I have never had such a present before or since! It thrills him because he loved seeing me unwrap a gift he gave to me in eternity past. I was born again on a warm August evening in 1945, but make no mistake about it, it was Christmas Day in heaven. I opened God's august gift to the anthems of angels (Luke 15:10).

FEELING GOD'S PLEASURE

My own effect before this personal God is to evoke his pleasure or cause him pain. In the Academy Award–winning film, *Chariots of Fire*, Eric Liddel, the Olympic athlete, refuses to run on Sunday because he feels this violation of the Sabbath will signal his disobedience to God. He chooses another kind of race on another day and becomes a gold medalist anyway. But his testament in the film is this: "When I run, I feel his pleasure." Looming up behind such a testament is love and grief. To grieve the heart of God is a serious thing. Liddel would rather lose on Saturday than win on Sunday. He was bent on feeling the pleasure of God.

> WHEN WE ARE BROKEN, WE ELICIT THE PLEASURE OF GOD. OUR CONTRITION ALWAYS PRECEDES OUR JOY.

I understand his need to bring pleasure to God. Since the day I was given the kingdom, I too have been absorbed in a race to win the pleasure of God. When I obey, I feel his pleasure. I once wrangled over God's call to preach in my life. My first two attempts at preaching were a disaster. I still recall the utter futility of trying to stand and speak in a confident way. I simply couldn't do it—it was embarrassing. After I decided I couldn't do it, for the next two years I wouldn't do it.

Finally, after two agonizing communication courses where I generally embarrassed the whole class with my ineptitude, I agreed to preach one Sunday morning at a small country church. My first Sunday in that pulpit began with a lot of self-abasement, but the further I "preached my way" into that first church sermon, the more confident I became. Even as I spoke, I sensed I was being obedient in doing what God seemed most to require. And though I was fearful, he poured down on me the riches of his rewards. My obedience brought his pleasure. His pleasure released the power within me to go on doing what I once believed I would never be able to do. So I had learned a great truth. When I obey him— particularly in the hard things he asks—I feel his pleasure. When I don't, I know that I have hurt him. When God is pleased, joy is possible and the power of his pleasure is mine.

CHAPTER TWO

• • • •

UNDERSTAND THAT YOUR OWN MOOD IS DETERMINED BY HOW GOD FEELS ABOUT YOU

● ● ● ●

It is God's goal that we become strong enough in spirit that the evil attacks of Satan and other people, and all the troubles of this life, become as nothing to us—falling to the ground with little effect as we become powerful and enduring in spirit. He wants our worth to be firmly based on the value he gives us, so that even when we are insulted to our face, our soul can say, "That's your opinion. I trust God alone to tell me what I'm worth." People who are growing strong in the Spirit of Christ can actually come to appreciate it when others speak evil of them—not because they like to be mistreated, but because it causes them to be more dependent on God for his word of approval. To live in his Presence is their only happiness.

—THOMAS À KEMPIS°

● ● ● ●

WALKING TO PLEASE GOD

The apostle Paul says that we should all walk to please God (1 Thessalonians 4:1). Why? Pleasing him should be the central duty of our discipleship. But hidden in our duty to God is the issue of our own well-being. God is a loving Father, and how he feels about us is how we feel about ourselves. Paul speaks of the pleasure of God four times, and each time he does so he uses the adjective *good* with it (Ephesians 1:5, 9; Philippians 2:13; 2 Thessalonians 1:11). The single time Jesus refers to the pleasure of God (Luke 12:32) he also uses the word *good*. Why is the pleasure of God so good? Because his pleasure toward us amounts to a therapy of joy.

We sometimes get things horribly mixed up in trying to hold on to both Jesus and the goodies of life. We don't need stuff to have joy and power. We need the pleasure of God. His smile always results in our joy. So most people—even most Christians, I'm afraid—spend their days trying to get all they can. Then they think they can enjoy all they get. But instead, they end up putting everything in a box; then they sit on the lid and poison the rest. Are such thing-centered Christians really joyful? Of course not! Their selfish drive to get ahead in the world steals from them the power of getting ahead in God's pleasure. They live weakly because they do not please God.

> **GOD'S PLEASURE TOWARD US AMOUNTS TO A THERAPY OF JOY.**

They are full of discord. Their lives produce no music.

Herman Hesse wrote what might be adopted as the creed of Christian power, for it is the creed of Christian joy: "You offer me flowers, yet I can live without flowers and many other things as well. But one thing I cannot and will not do without: I can never live as much as a single day in which the music in my heart is not dominant."[7] Joy is the great imperative of the Christian experience. Joy is essential to living the Christian life. But the soul can only be taught to sing by the pleasure of God.

God's pleasure bequeaths a double joy. The first joy it gives us is the power to face all things. This power allows us to be achievers. And because we feel that through our achievements God has given us the upper hand in redeeming his world, we receive the second joy—we become people of confidence. Our achievements are never our doing. They come from our joyful dependency on him. And our dependency leads to confidence in what we can do through him.

SETTLING INTO THE RHYTHM OF DELIVERANCE

Many of us suffer from low self-esteem. This low mood is sponsored by the feeling that we are not achieving anything of value in our career dreams or in our striving after fulfillment. Often such low self-opinions come because we so consistently disappoint ourselves. Low self-esteem may come after we have found no power in the latest best-seller on how to be number one in the workplace.

There exists the notion that to feel good about ourselves we must compete until we actually do begin to win more often than we lose. We have been led to believe that when we stand on top of those we vanquish, they will have to look up to us, and we will have to look up to no one. Yet the most miserable of people are often those deceived conquerors whose conquests leave them at last on top of the world still holding a shaky opinion of themselves.

Striving to be number one only wraps us more tightly in the package of ourselves. It gives us an erroneous view of life. We come to see the world only in terms of ourselves. It seems to us the world exists to make us happy, to challenge us, or to provide us a reputation. The world, as Shakespeare's character Pistol said, is our oyster. But the Cross stands at our entrance to that world and firmly challenges us with this question: "Is the world a worthy oyster? When you've eaten and digested it, does it satisfy you for long?" It is easy to give the world our routines and settle into its cadence. But Kazanzakis reminds us, "Only he who obeys a rhythm superior to his own is free."[8]

But how do we find this rhythm of deliverance? We start at the center of our emptiness. We confess freely that our hearts are the unworthy temples for the adoration of our egos. We admit that we were foolish to become ensnared by our old routines, rhythms, and selfish dreams of fulfillment. When we put aside the rhythm of self, we are free to be swept up in the rhythm of God's joy.

THE JOY OF CONFESSION

One wonders if the thief on the cross isn't an existential disappointment to himself. He must have once had dreams for getting ahead. All of us do. His mother and father must have once believed in him. Perhaps his wife and children. But his ego is now displaced by a naked, bleeding emptiness. His dreams sag out from the wood, and all that he thought he might once have accomplished is lost. His one last hope is to release the tight little bundle of ego in which he has always wrapped himself and then cry with his last breath, "Lord, will you remember me when you come into your kingdom?"

STRIVING TO BE NUMBER ONE ONLY WRAPS US MORE TIGHTLY IN THE PACKAGE OF OURSELVES. IT GIVES US AN ERRONEOUS VIEW OF LIFE.

Now at last he is empty of the sin that brought him to execution. Now his skewered heart is poured out. He is clean. His shame-washed ego has drained away. In rushes substance! God is pleased. Those around his cross must have marveled that a dying man could wear such a winning smile. But then that is what confession does. It is a double axe that cuts the feet from our pointless journeys and the head from our flighty pride.

Confession is God's gift to us, to help us empty ourselves of self. Confession pulls the plug on ego, draining from our lives all that was most obnoxious—us! Does the constant focus on ourselves provide us with happiness? Hardly. We are the disappointing focus of our powerless altars. We almost never achieve all that we wanted to and especially on the time-table we had set for ourselves.

THE JOY OF "FAILURE"

Twice in Scripture God says that he was pleased with Jesus. One of these affirmations of God's pleasure in Christ came at his baptism (Matthew 3:17); the other came at his transfiguration (Matthew 17:5). Have you ever wondered how Christ could go to the cross and follow the divine course of dying while never voicing one protest to his humiliation? I believe that Jesus had heard God on these occasions say how pleased he was with his Son. The Father's pleasure then afforded Christ a completed view of who he was and why he was in the world. On the cross he didn't look like a person in charge of his destiny. But Jesus knew that God was pleased, and his appearance to his crucifiers was of no importance.

Every day may not bring a cross, but it will surely offer us a bump or two. And within each day is a reason to lament or rejoice. There is plenty of pain there. The philosopher reminds us that into every life a little rain must fall. The songwriter reminds us that those raindrops keep falling on our heads. And the physicist reminds us that the terminal velocity of a raindrop is twenty-two miles per hour. They do indeed hurt when they hit. But there are umbrellas in the world. Surely God has within himself the power to protect us. When we obey, he smiles. Feeling his pleasure puts the power within us. Then the rain may be conquered or ignored.

Once we know that God takes pleasure in our obedience, little else matters. Our self-esteem rarely flags. When God is okay, we are okay. Our circumstances then do not determine how we feel about ourselves. Esther, in her moment of crisis, could say, "Though it is against the law, I will go in to see the king. If I must die, I am willing to die" (Esther 4:16). There is a power to go about doing right, and our success or failure is not part of the equation. In fact, we are freed from the bondage of always having to feel like we're getting ahead. If we succeed, the glory is his. If we fail, he is pleased when we try again. And when he is pleased, we cannot fail.

If God is served, what appears to be failure may be the most glorious of successes. The cross was the heavy work of obedience, and it looked to the world like the ultimate failure. But Jesus' obedience in execution brought to God the smile of pleasure. How does Jesus feel about himself?

He has no inordinate pride. He knew who he was and what he was here to do.

> IF WE FAIL, GOD IS PLEASED WHEN WE TRY AGAIN. AND WHEN HE IS PLEASED, WE CANNOT FAIL.

From Esther and Jesus we clearly see the power of God's pleasure. Or we can examine three Hebrew children, Shadrach, Meshach, and Abednego, about to be thrown into the fiery furnace. Nebuchadnezzar challenged them in this way: "I will give you one more chance. If you bow down and worship the statue I have made when you hear the sound of the musical instruments, all will be well. But if you refuse, you will be thrown immediately into the blazing furnace. What god will be able to rescue you from my power then?" But these three gallants facing martyrdom seem altogether settled in their minds as they reply: "O Nebuchadnezzar, we do not need to defend ourselves before you. If we are thrown into the blazing furnace, the God whom we serve is able to save us. He will rescue us from your power, Your Majesty. But even if he doesn't, Your Majesty can be sure that we will never serve your gods or worship the gold statue you have set up" (Daniel 3:15-18).

In all these cases the pleasure of God kept those who faced crises exulting in victory. Knowing that God was pleased kept them from feeling any sense of personal loss. Their obedience had caused them to abdicate their egos. God smiled. The power of his pleasure was theirs.

● ● ● ●

CHAPTER THREE

REALIZE THAT
THE POWER FOR LIVING
IS THE PRODUCT OF
GOD'S PLEASURE

❀ ❀ ❀ ❀

Eyes of my soul, ye have no need to wait until the veil of the flesh that screens off the beatific vision has been rent in twain by the mighty hands of the Angel of Death, ere ye behold the land that floweth with milk and honey!

Ears of my heart, ye need not remain dull and listless till the peal of the archangel's trumpet thrill you, and summon you to the music of the harpers harping on their harps or the chime of the glassy sea.

Heart of mine, be expectant! Awake! Lo, there shall come into thee, penetrating, pervading, filling thy every recess, all those blessed things which God hath prepared for them that love Him. They shall enter thee, as a retinue of knights might enter a beleaguered castle to make it strong against any possible combination of the foe.

—F. B. MEYER[9]

❀ ❀ ❀ ❀

THE JOY OF SERVICE

The gifts of the Spirit are not just little "occupational" gifts to make the church "work" or to keep us "busy" within our church community, as if serving God were an alternative to softball. These spiritual gifts are areas of service that God has given us to perform, and our performance of them brings God pleasure. To fail to know what our gifts are will keep us wandering around for a lifetime, not knowing what God has given us to do to please him. Only when we learn what we are to do and begin doing it—and keep on doing it—will we ever serve our world as God intended. Until we are doing what God has gifted us to do, we will not be doing what God has called us to do. His gifts are given unto us to furnish us to do his calling. So we have not the slightest chance to tap into the service of God's pleasure (See Romans 12, 1 Corinthians 12, and Ephesians 4) until we are using his gifts to achieve his calling in our lives. It all adds up to ministry. Therefore, until we minister to our world, we have not the slightest opportunity of bringing joy to ourselves.

There's an old anonymous English carol in which Jesus seems to be throwing a great ball for all the members of his church. And in this song Jesus is the Lord of the Dance as he sings these words:

Tomorrow shall be my dancing day;
I would my true love did so chance
To see the legend of my play,
To call my true love to my dance.

Then was I born of a virgin pure,
Of her I took fleshly substance;
Thus was I knit to man's nature
To call my true love to my dance.

In a manger laid and wrapped I was,
So very poor, this was my chance
Betwixt an ox and a silly poor ass,

To call my true love to my dance.

Then afterwards baptized I was;
The Holy Ghost on me did glance,
My father's voice heard from above,
To call my true love to my dance.

Sing, O my love,
O my love, my love, my love;
This have I done for my true love.

God takes pleasure in seeing us, his children, care about what he wants us to do. What are we doing to minister in his world? The gifts of the Spirit outlined in these passages (Romans 12, 1 Corinthians 12, and Ephesians 4) have to do with serving others. Until we care about the plight of others, we haven't the slightest chance of gaining God's pleasure, because service is the primary evidence of our obedience. Jesus made it clear that he came not to be "ministered unto but to minister, and to give his life as a ransom for many" (Matthew

20:28, KJV). Furthermore, said Jesus, "whoever desires to be great among you will be your servant (Mark 10:43, NKJV).

Albert Schweitzer, a twentieth century founder of hospitals in Africa, was asked to name the greatest person alive in the world at that very moment. He said that the greatest person alive at that moment was an unknown person, living in some obscure place, who had gone to some needy person in the name of love to do some necessary thing no one else was doing.[10] At every moment of ministry, God smiles and heaven whispers, "In as much as you have done it unto one of the least of these my brothers you have done it unto me." Why is it so important to do loving things in the name of Christ? Because, said Kierkegaard,

> UNTIL WE ARE DOING WHAT GOD HAS GIFTED US TO DO, WE WILL NOT BE DOING WHAT GOD HAS CALLED US TO DO.

"to love another person is to help them love God."

Such acts of service do not have to be grand. One day I was having dinner with a friend of mine who is a stroke victim. Her left arm is nearly useless. We were eating and chatting casually when I noticed she was trying to "chop up" her baked potato with only one hand. Without speaking I simply reached across the table and placed my index finger and middle finger on one end of her potato to stop its skidding about her plate. She quickly cut it into eatable sections. Then she lifted her eyes and smiled at me. But God's smile was the one I felt. Even the tiniest acts of love may win the grandest smile of God.

Acts of service that please God do not necessarily have to be done by Christians. God is pleased by humble obedience, wherever it's found. God is pleased by simple acts of service. At a fast-food restaurant in the Pacific Northwest a man in the drive-thru lane bought a cup of coffee for the driver of the car behind him. He didn't know the next driver in line, but the coffee cost him only eighty-nine cents. It was human enough to say, "Hi! I'm on my way to work too. Let's be fellow human beings together." The message was enough to create a matrix of compassion. The clerk said that the custom of buying an extra cup of coffee for the driver of "the next car back" continued for two hours and twenty-seven customers![11]

> ACTS OF SERVICE THAT PLEASE GOD DO NOT HAVE TO BE GRAND. THEY DON'T EVEN NECESSARILY HAVE TO BE DONE BY CHRISTIANS.

It is not often that a fast-food chain illustrates the power of pleasure, but the joy of it all must have continued for the rest of the day. It could be argued that all of those in the drive-thru lane weren't Christians seeking to be obedient. True. But remember what James said: "Every good gift and every perfect gift is from above, and comes down from the Father." (1:17, NKJV). God's pleasure falls broadly on all human kindness. Merely being "human" in the best sense of the word elicits the pleasure of God. The power of such pleasure set a great number of people free that day.

WINNING GOD'S SMILE

God has made the Christian life in such a way that we can derive power from the pleasure of obedience. This force is achieved as we take our lives out of the center of things. Our own egos are dethroned to make way for God to occupy the ruling chair in the center of our souls. To don the apron and pick up the basin to wash the feet of all the needy God sends our way is tantamount to winning his smile.

I spoke at a large church banquet recently. Dr. B., the pastor, was working in the kitchen, washing and scrubbing dishes right along with the cleanup crew. None there saw his Ph.D. as an impediment to genuine humility. He was gathering the smile of God.

Such simple obedience and service wins the smile of God. It also keeps us from getting too wrapped up in ourselves. So it delivers us from self-centeredness as it gives us the joy of serving others. But the last, greatest benefit comes as we receive his smile and are empowered by his pleasure.

PLEASING GOD WITH OUR WHOLE LIVES

So we have come full circle from the start of our study. At the beginning I said that the most futile of all pursuits is the pursuit of pleasure. Now we can clearly see that the futility of trying to be happy by serving ourselves is neurotic work. But when we lose ourselves in serving others, we find happiness from the power of God's pleasure.

Yet how few Christians bypass this neurosis! Many of us come to Christ believing that Christianity exists to make us happy. After all, didn't the evangelist say, "Accept Jesus and you will be happy?" So, we "accept" Jesus. Then, by the following Thursday, we are haunted by the blahs. "If Jesus is my Savior," we're tempted to ask ourselves, "why am I not still a bucket of pink?" Think about it. Do we really believe that Jesus died to keep us delirious for the rest of our lives? How false! He died to save us from our most basic sin—the sin of putting ourselves before God. And in so doing he taught us that obedience wins the smile of God. Christ died to show us that pleasing God comes only in our service. Jesus isn't the goody-box that replaces our old self-help books.

Further, Jesus doesn't just sanctify our religious life. Instead he empowers the life that we are called upon to live outside the church. Perhaps this is the greatest danger for those who become Christians as adults. We cherish our salvation, but rarely see that our conversion—our having given all to Christ—has anything to do with what we do to earn a living. We do in a fashion give ourselves to Jesus, but we rarely ask if he has any lordship requirements as to our salaried jobs. Thus, we never really consider the idea that we should be pleasing God with the totality of our lives.

We seem to believe that to please God is to regularly attend Sunday school or to go to church once a week. We don't consider other areas of our lives part of our service to God. Once we get to church or get off work, *then* we will serve. Thus a large part of our lives is "off limits" to the power of God's pleasure.

We can please God and release his pleasure only if we see that *all* of our life is the arena of his will. We are most healthy when there is no sacred or leisure side to all he calls us to do. We must live holistically. Every waking moment is the ongoing forum of his pleasure.

SCRUBBING JOY

Still we must not trivialize God or his great will. Vast dreams of ministry and mission—great God-sized visions—become the best center of our devotion to serve God's immense plan of world redemption. Our lives will command God's greatest pleasure only when we live with such all-consuming vision. How meaningful it is for us. Still, God's pleasure is spent in less grand ways.

The point is that whether we focus on great dreams or smaller ones, we must always elevate our sense of God's will. We need not busy our hearts with the mundane and trivial. Our lives must remain focused on the issues God has for us to pursue. Issues of life direction, career pursuits, areas of ministry, self-improvement. Key issues of the heart's obedience must be our focus. With that as our main course, we need not concern ourselves as to whether God approves of the condiments we use or whether we have chosen the proper teacup to please him. Still even those times when we must take care of the mundane things of life can become occasions for us to strengthen our inner life by an unbroken focus on our love for him.

WE CAN PLEASE GOD AND RELEASE HIS PLEASURE ONLY IF WE SEE THAT ALL OF OUR LIFE IS THE ARENA OF HIS WILL.

We have already pointed out that Brother Lawrence scrubbed pots in a monastery kitchen. He did not glory in the scrubbing as a *way* to praise. But he did glory in such mundane work as an *opportunity* to praise. The grime of his hands was not the goal, for it only distracted his hands, leaving his heart free to continue to sing its *Te Deum*s in praise before the throne of God. His menial work afforded him singing room at the throne of God. Thus there was nothing that could prevent him from continuing to appropriate the power of God's pleasure. Then the pleasure of heaven brought joy to the dishwater, and the marriage of pleasure and joy elevated his living.

Teresa of Avila confessed that God did not want "nuns who were ninnies." Further, she said, God had no use for frowning saints. How often I have discovered that the church is full of frowning saints. I can only surmise that we have missed Brother Lawrence's path to pleasure. We have begrudged the scrubbing of pots as a hell to be escaped rather than a heaven to be enjoyed. In a larger context, Brother Lawrence's scrubbing joy becomes a way of life to all who cherish the gifts of the Spirit. They are the scrub work of God.

MASKING PRETEND PRAYER
WITH FALSE JOY

All of us have noticed that the church is a place of wonderful relationships, but it can also be a citadel of "ouchy" relationships.

I used to be a pastor, and I learned early that I could not celebrate all the "Christians" I knew. Some of them seemed Christlike, but many of them seemed Lucifer-like. How could they stand in worship and sing so sweetly about the Jesus they seemed so little like? I learned from some of these poorer disciples that we can pretend a joy we never really own. We can mask ourselves with joy, while harboring our fanged and individual grudges. Whatever we dour disciples look like we are singing, we are really singing:

> To live above with saints we love,
>> Oh that will be the glory!
> But, to live below with saints we know,
>> Well that's a different story!

Pretense in prayer is a common activity in our churches. Real prayer ends in the pleasure of God and the joy of the believer. The other ends in dyspepsia and a continual rehearsal of the happiness act. In short, those who engage in pretend prayer are always wearing a mask. Helen Joseph must have met some of these ritual actors of godliness, for she wrote:

"Always a mask,
    Held in the hand whitely,
Always she had a mask before her face—
Smiling and uprightly,
    The mask.
For years I wondered
But dared not ask
And then—
I blundered,
I looked behind the mask,
To find
nothing—
She had no face.
She had become merely a hand
Holding the mask
With grace.
    —HELEN JOSEPH[12]

The mask is the way many of us in churches often substitute pretense for authenticity. It is always a way we tend to keep a spiritual reputation while living the most secular lives possible.

> AUTHENTICITY WINS THE SMILE OF GOD. WEAKNESS LIES IN PRETENSE.

But in the pretense lies our weakness. Authenticity wins the smile of God. This means that even in our seasons of depression, when we can't seem to find God, we must not pretend to be happy or triumphant to trump up some impression of inner power. Rather, we must go to God candidly confessing our whipped spirit and begging him to remind us that the path out of our defeat lies in catching his view of us.

CHERISHING YOUR NEED

One of the darkest days of my life was when I was interviewed by a very prestigious seminary who had given me every assurance they were going to hire me. Then, in a bureaucratic turn of events, they told me I could not have the job they had all but assured me I would get. I suffered an immense loss of face since I had told all my friends and acquaintances I would soon be teaching on that faculty.

I was broken and whipped. I could not go in before the Lord with any of my own self-esteem. My hurt was so grievous, I crawled into the throne room and confessed to God that the darkness beyond me was only excelled by the darkness within me.

But my honesty about my broken spirit was just the entrance God needed to remind me that brokenness, with the self-recrimination that attends it, is just the place where God publishes his view of us. He touched my brokenness with his approval and succored my wounds with his broad smile.

Could it be that I—self-loathing and stripped of any self-esteem—could bring him pleasure?

Indeed!

And his pleasure made me whole. I healed up in his presence. His pleasure in my honest need was a therapy of power. I healed. I became strong. I was filled with the power to stand and bless his name.

So cherish your need! There is a better call!

There is a higher view of who you are!

There is a greater power!

Be honest before God and that power will be born in you.

● ● ● ●

CONCLUSION
JOY: THE EVIDENCE OF THE POWER OF HIS PLEASURE

◉ ◉ ◉ ◉

Imagine how the disciples were feeling that morning as they started on their journey. Their hearts were sad and troubled because they thought that Jesus was dead. They did not know that he was alive, and this is the way it is with a large number of Christians. They look to the Cross and they struggle to trust Christ, but they have never yet learned the blessedness of believing that there is a living Christ who will do everything for them. The words that the angel spoke to the women who came to Christ's tomb on the morning of the Resurrection were striking: "Why seek ye the living among the dead?" (Luke 24:5). What is the difference between a dead Christ, whom the women had gone to anoint, and a living Christ? The difference is that I must do everything for a dead Christ, but a living Christ does everything for me.

—ANDREW MURRAY[13]

◉ ◉ ◉ ◉

When Jesus was baptized, God spoke in a loud voice saying, "You are my beloved Son, and I am fully pleased with you." (Luke 3:22). The three years that followed the voice over the river were the most remarkable three years in history. Christ, single-handedly, thriving on the pleasure of the Father, accomplished our redemption. We can and should credit all that Christ did on our behalf to his holiness and his sinlessness, but we must not overlook the wonder of his single-minded pursuit of his Father's pleasure.

Jesus was incapable of arrogance, for he never existed for his own reasons. He came to earth for one reason, to serve the pleasure of his Father's will. Such power had never before been given to anyone. But now that same power is available to us! In fact, in speaking of his own acts of power, Jesus said, "The truth is, anyone who believes in me will do the same works I have done, and even greater works, because I am going to be with the Father. You can ask for anything in my name, and I will do it, because the work of the Son brings glory to the Father" (John 14:12-13).

His power is now ours.

Jesus said to the disciples, "I have given you authority over all the power of the enemy, and you can walk among snakes and scorpions and crush them" (Luke 10:19). Then he set his Holy Spirit in us to accomplish all we attempt so that we might bring glory to Christ. In glorifying Christ, we please the Father. When we please the Father, he gives us yet more power. Then we surge forward to please him once again. So the pleasure and the power come in this never-ending cycle. We live in a grand rhythm of glory.

OUR POWER TO LIVE ABOVE OUR CIRCUMSTANCES IS THE PHENOMENON OF GOD'S PLEASURE.

God is pleased when this ever-cycling rhythm of life makes us pictures of self-confidence and power. James A. Harnish asks the

most central question concerning our lives of
ministry:

> Where do you find the power to hang
> in there in this world?
> Where do you find the power to keep
> going
> when the going really gets tough?
> Where do you find the power to continue
> to work for peace
> in a world that is addicted to violence?
> Where do we find the power to continue
> to believe in good in a world that is filled
> with so much suffering and pain?
> Where do we find the power to continue
> to believe that ultimately God's Kingdom
> will come
> and God's will, as revealed in Jesus, will
> be done in all creation?
> Where do we find the power to be a
> disciple of Jesus in this world?
> —JAMES A. HARNISH[14]

Our power to live above our circumstances is the phenomenon of God's pleasure. When he smiles, we can do it. Until he smiles, we are weak and powerless. Name any soul who has altered or beautified the course of Christian history, and you will see two things: a person of obedience, and a servant who owned the power of God's pleasure.

None of these ever took credit for what they achieved. They were not after credit. They sought to win the pleasure of God. When he smiled, they felt the energy of heaven rising in their souls. The Bible says that early Christians turned the world upside down (Acts 17:6). They did—but not because they found any pleasure in world-turning. They believed that God, for reasons of his own, wanted the world inverted by seeing the world converted. So they did what Archimedes could not: they took the lever of salvation and pried the world from paganism to faith. They pleased God in this, and he daily furnished them with the power to get his will done.

A great violinist played a Haydn concerto in a full theater. The music was good and the audience was rapt. But the violinist was uninterested in audience rapture. His eyes swept the darkened corners of the balcony. Over the fret and bow, over the glistening strings, he cast his furtive glances toward only one patron. There sat his teacher of many years. His was the only pleasure that mattered. Was the old man smiling? Was he frowning? Then the stingy light moved up, and the darkness retreated. For one single instance the student saw the gleaming teeth, the broad face, the wide smile.

Then the power fell.

The music owned the world.

The dance had been called for by the Lord of the Dance:

"Then afterwards baptized I was,
The Holy Ghost on me did glance

My Father's voice heard from above,
To call my true love to the dance."

The Master is pleased, and in his pleasure is
the power.

Smile on me, O God, and the world I
could not conquer shall be yours this very
hour.

The dragon who once flew at me in fire
    lies flameless, spent, and cold.
And I, the weakest of all souls,
    will lift a victory of gold.
And lay at your feet, O God.
    You have only to smile and you
      will see
Your pleasure is a force to free:
    The power of Christ who
      strengthens me.

NOTES

1. Menachem Begin, in *Bartlett's Familiar Quotations*, ed. Justin Kaplan (NY: Little, Brown and Company, 1992) , 732.9-10.
2. David Hansen, *Long Wandering Prayer* (Downers Grove, IL: InterVarsity Press, 2001), 158-159.
3. Edward Sanford Martin, in Leonard Sweet, *A Cup of Coffee at the Soul Café* (Nashville, TN: Broadman & Holman Publishers, 1998), 27.
4. Brother Lawrence, *The Practice of the Presence of God*, Fifth Letter.
5. Jonathan Edwards, in David Hansen, *Long Wandering Prayer* (Downers Grove, IL: InterVarsity Press, 2001), 42.
6. Thomas à Kempis, *Come, Lord Jesus*, ed. David Hazard (Minneapolis, MN: Bethany House Publishers, 1999), 146.
7. Herman Hesse, in Leonard Sweet, *A Cup of Coffee at the Soul Café* (Nashville, TN: Broadman & Holman Publishers, 1998), 69.
8. Robert Benson, *Living Prayer* (New York: Tarcher Putnam, 1998), 14.

9. F.B. Meyer, *Our Daily Homily* (London: Marshall Morgan & Scott, 1951), 135.

10. Albert Schweitzer, in Leonard Sweet, *A Cup of Coffee at the Soul Café* (Nashville, TN: Broadman & Holman Publishers, 1998), 34.

11. Glen Zander as quoted on www.preachingtoday.com.

12. Helen Joseph, in Leonard Sweet, *A Cup of Coffee at the Soul Café* (Nashville, TN: Broadman & Holman Publishers, 1998), 17.

13. Andrew Murray, *The Secret of Spiritual Strength* (New Kensington, PA: Whitaker House, 1997), 11.

14. James A. Harnish, in Leonard Sweet, *A Cup of Coffee at the Soul Café* (Nashville, TN: Broadman & Holman Publishers, 1998), 50.